picture

horse

frog

clock

teddy bear

boots

chair

umbrella

rug

bridge

train

animals

car

basket

ball

telephone

shoes

ISBN 0 86112 753 6
© Brimax Books Ltd 1992. All rights reserved.
Published by Brimax Books Ltd, Newmarket, England 1992.
Reprinted 1995
Printed in Spain.

My First
500 words

Illustrated by Stephanie Ryder

toy box

boat

book

socks

BRIMAX • NEWMARKET • ENGLAND

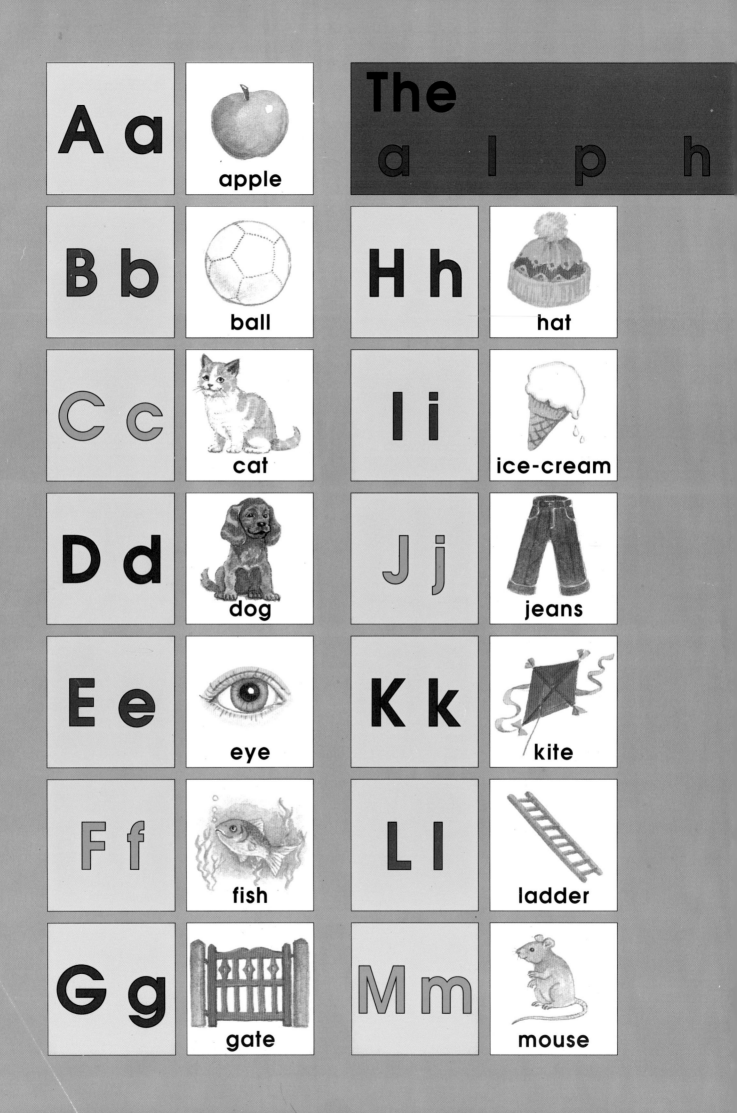

The alph

A a — apple

B b — ball

C c — cat

D d — dog

E e — eye

F f — fish

G g — gate

H h — hat

I i — ice-cream

J j — jeans

K k — kite

L l — ladder

M m — mouse

a b e t

N n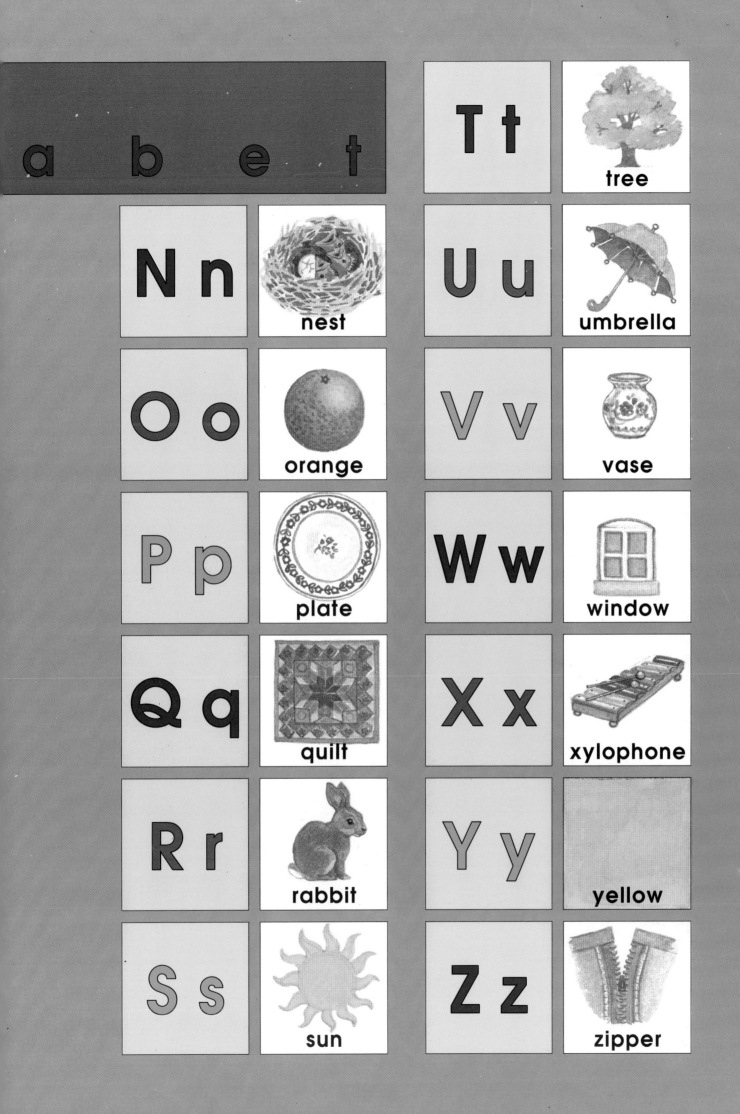
nest

O o
orange

P p
plate

Q q
quilt

R r
rabbit

S s
sun

T t
tree

U u
umbrella

V v
vase

W w
window

X x
xylophone

Y y
yellow

Z z
zipper

1 one

2 two

3 three

4 four

5 five

6 six

7 seven

8 eight

9 nine

10 ten

11 eleven

12 twelve

13 thirteen

14 fourteen

15 fifteen

16 sixteen

17 seventeen

18 eighteen

19 nineteen

20 twenty

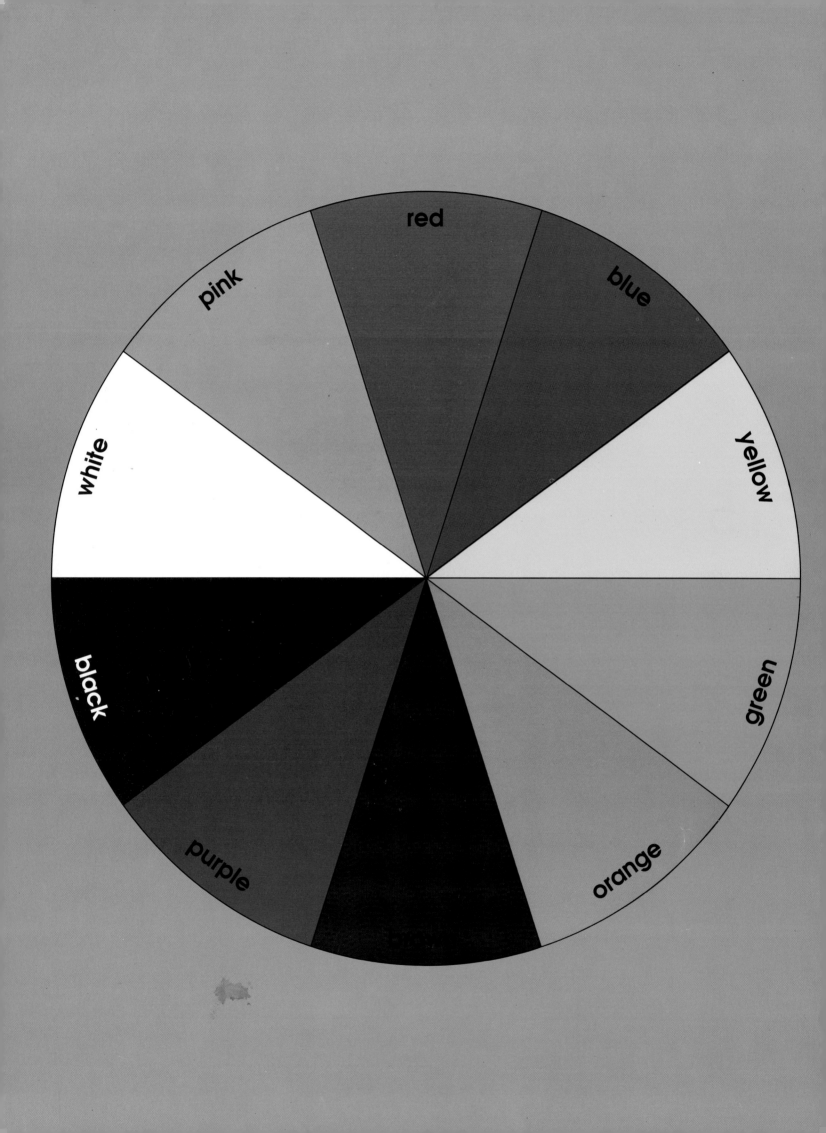

red car

brown dog

blue kite

purple scarf

yellow sun

black cat

green bicycle

white cloud

orange hat

pink flower

Monday

Tuesday

Wednesday

Thursday

Friday

Saturday

Sunday

Spring

Winter

Summer

Autumn

January

February

March

April

May

June

July

August

September

October

November

December

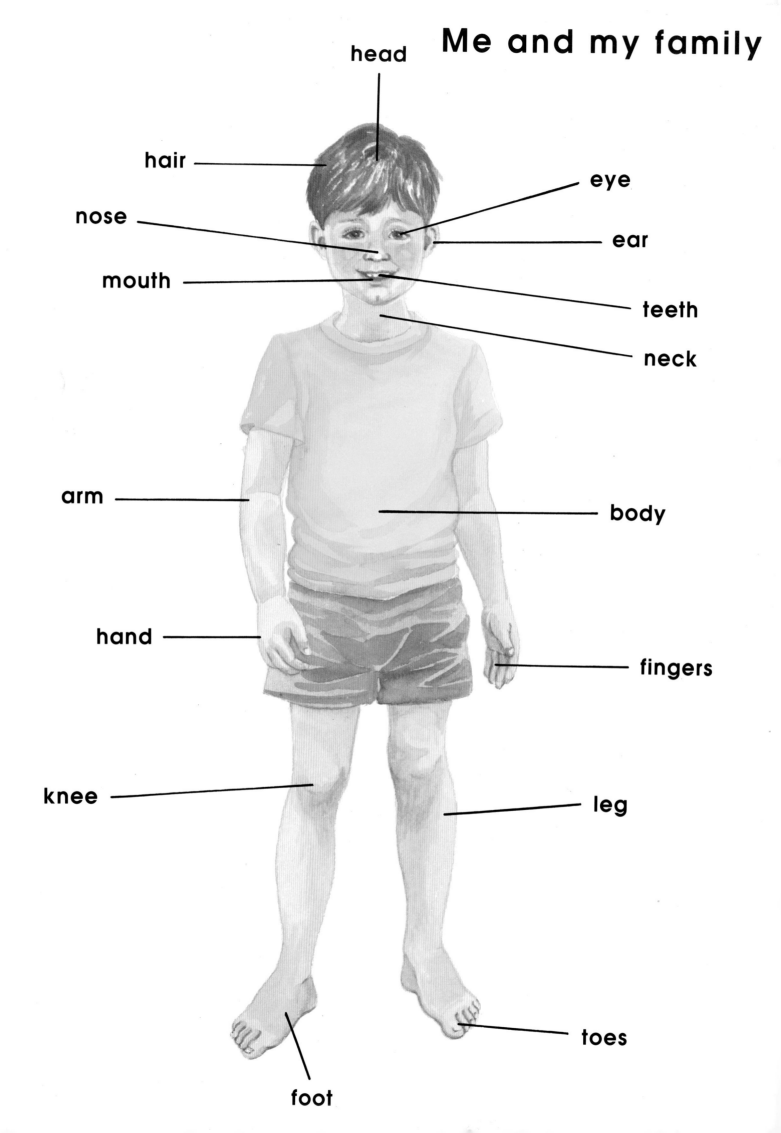

Me and my family

head

hair

nose

mouth

eye

ear

teeth

neck

arm

body

hand

fingers

knee

leg

toes

foot

uncle

mother

father

grandpa

sister

aunt

brother

cousins

baby

grandma

big	**small**
a big elephant	a small mouse
inside	**outside**
inside the house	outside the house
happy	**sad**
a happy face	a sad face
hot	**cold**
hot soup	cold ice-cream
wet	**dry**
wet raindrops	an umbrella to keep me dry
fast	**slow**
a fast rabbit	a slow snail
up	**down**
up the stairs	down the stairs
over	**under**
over the bridge	under the bridge
day	**night**
a sunny day	a dark night
hard	**soft**
a hard rock	a soft pillow

circle

square

diamond

star

triangle

Animals

koala

kangaroo

camel

gorilla

tiger

zebra

turtle

crocodile

hippopotamus

rhinoceros

lion

monkey

iguana

fox

giraffe

beaver

elephant

raccoon

snake

polar bear

bear

panda

Pets

pony

rabbit

canary

tortoise

goldfish

dog

cat

mice

hamster

guinea pig

Birds

parrot

peacock

pigeon

penguin

eagle

vulture

ostrich

swan

shoes

dress

blouse

socks

hat

skirt

jeans

coat

sweater

t-shirt

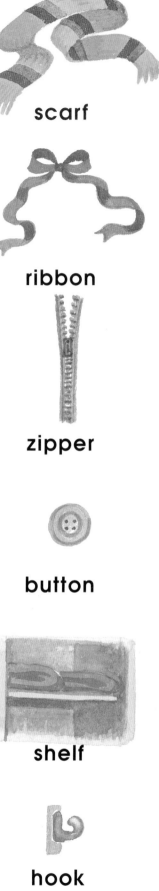

scarf

ribbon

zipper

button

shelf

hook

jacket

trousers

shorts

drawer

hanger

Learn and play

paint brush

picture

scissors

paint

pencil

chalk

blackboard

clock

apron

cloth

sandbox

glue

dinosaur

fingerpaint

desk

crayon

paper

bucket

flag

beachball

ship

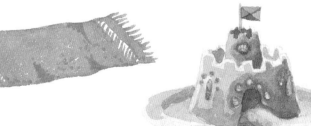

towel   sandcastle   seagull   starfish

ice-cream

rock

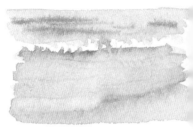

sea

hat

crab

shell

lighthouse

sand

Shopping

bread

eggs

milk

cheese

potatoes

oranges

apples

meat

grapes

sausages

tomatoes

basket

purse

money

bag

carrots

chocolate

bananas

doctor

nurse

spoon

thermometer

Band-Aid ™

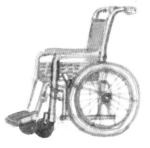

wheelchair

stethoscope

scissors

medicine

bandage

cream

In the garden

watering can

flower

hose

cabbage

sprinkler

flower pot

wheel barrow

lawnmower

cat

grass

trees

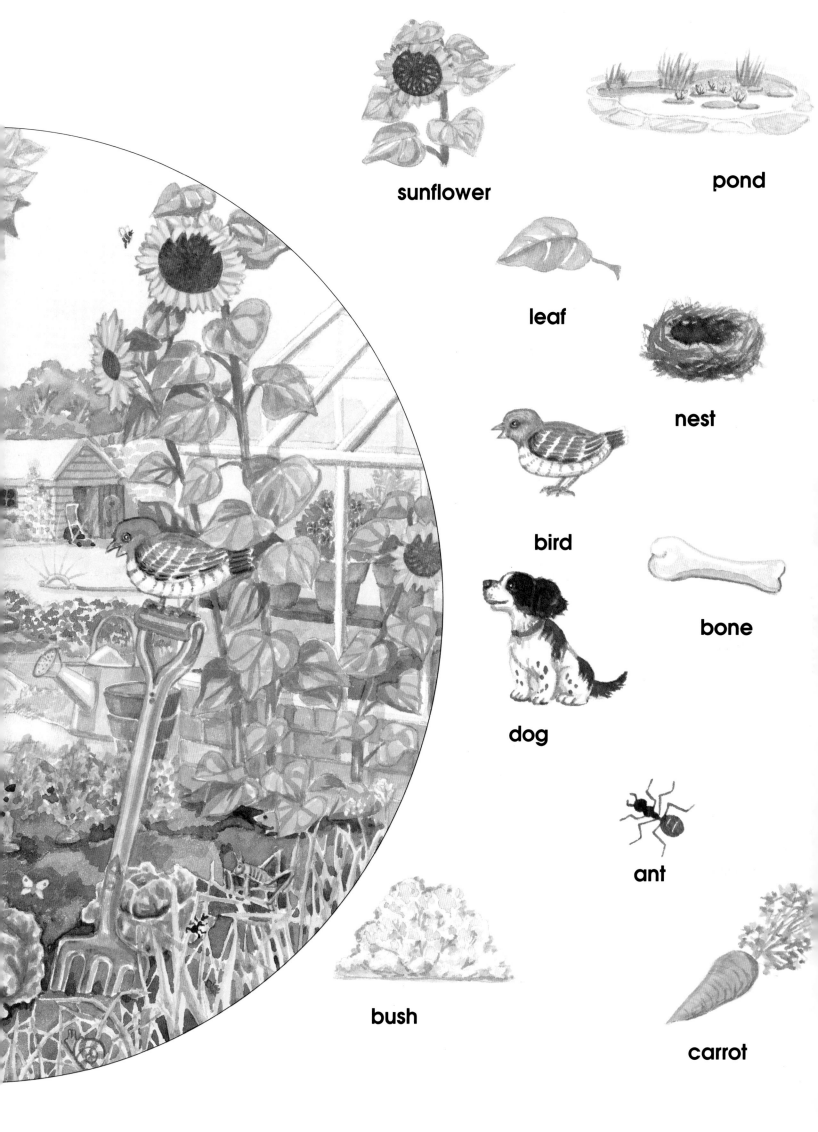

sunflower

pond

leaf

nest

bird

bone

dog

ant

bush

carrot

jack-in
the-box

doll

teddy bear

train

jig-saw
puzzle

car

drum

book

plane

rocking horse

truck

ball

yo-yo

track

blocks

clown

trumpet

helicopter

tunnel

puddle

boots

A rainy day

rainbow

frog

bridge

boat

umbrella

cloud

wheel

fence

wall

tent

train

plane

raincoat

rain hat

tractor

pig

chick

goat

lamb

duck

horse

scarecrow   cow

feathers

bucket

turkey

goose

pond

farmer

stable

barn

ice skates

snowman

Playing in the snow

skis

gloves

scarf

mittens

snowballs

icicles

hat

robin

pipe

mountain

coat

jacket

snowflake

iceberg

igloo

eskimo

toboggan

trees

hammer

toolbox

nail

paint

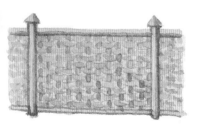

fence

Working outside

ladder

window

garage

broom

cobweb

spider

path

chimney

axe

car

house

roof

door

A birthday party

cake

balloon

straw

cookie

candle

presents

ice-cream

party hat

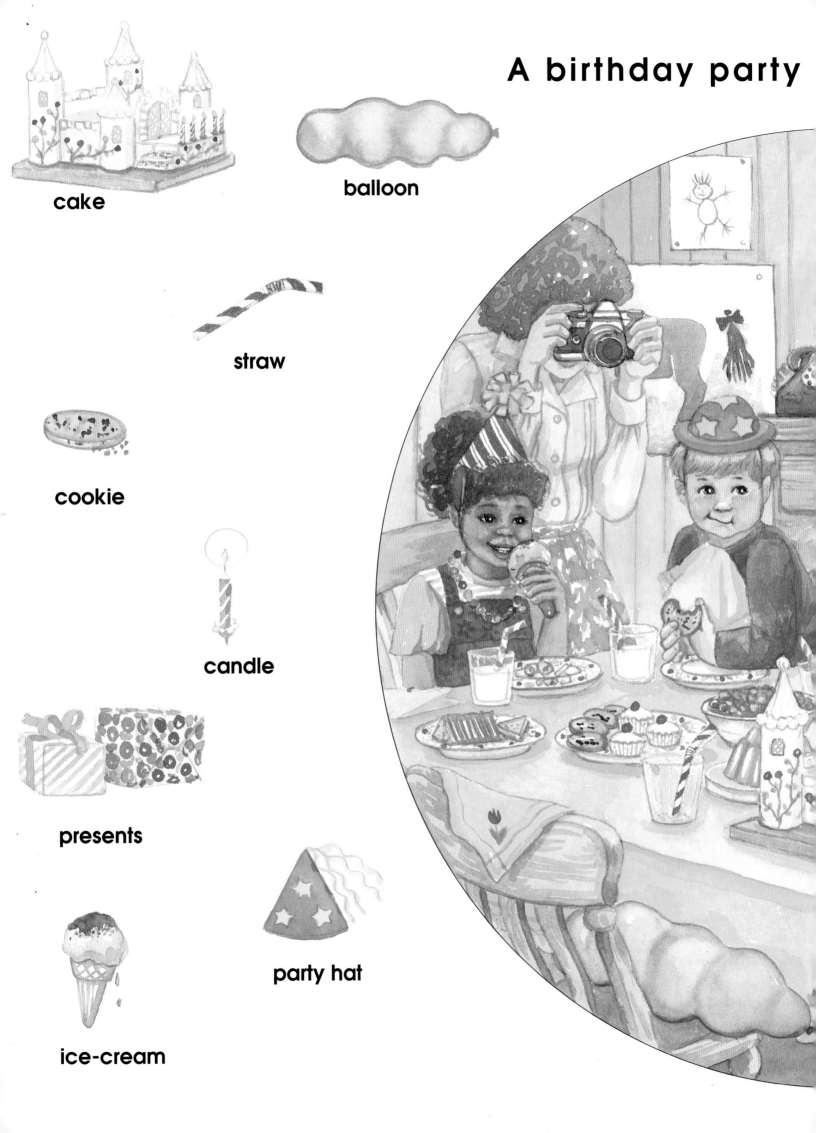

telephone

milk

necklace

cards

camera

napkin

tablecloth

table

chair

In the kitchen

stove

flour

butter

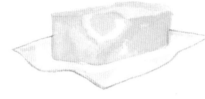

mixing bowl

eggs

rolling pin

apron

wooden spoon

table

plate

toaster

microwave

saucepan

chair

sink

cup

knife

spoon

fork

glass

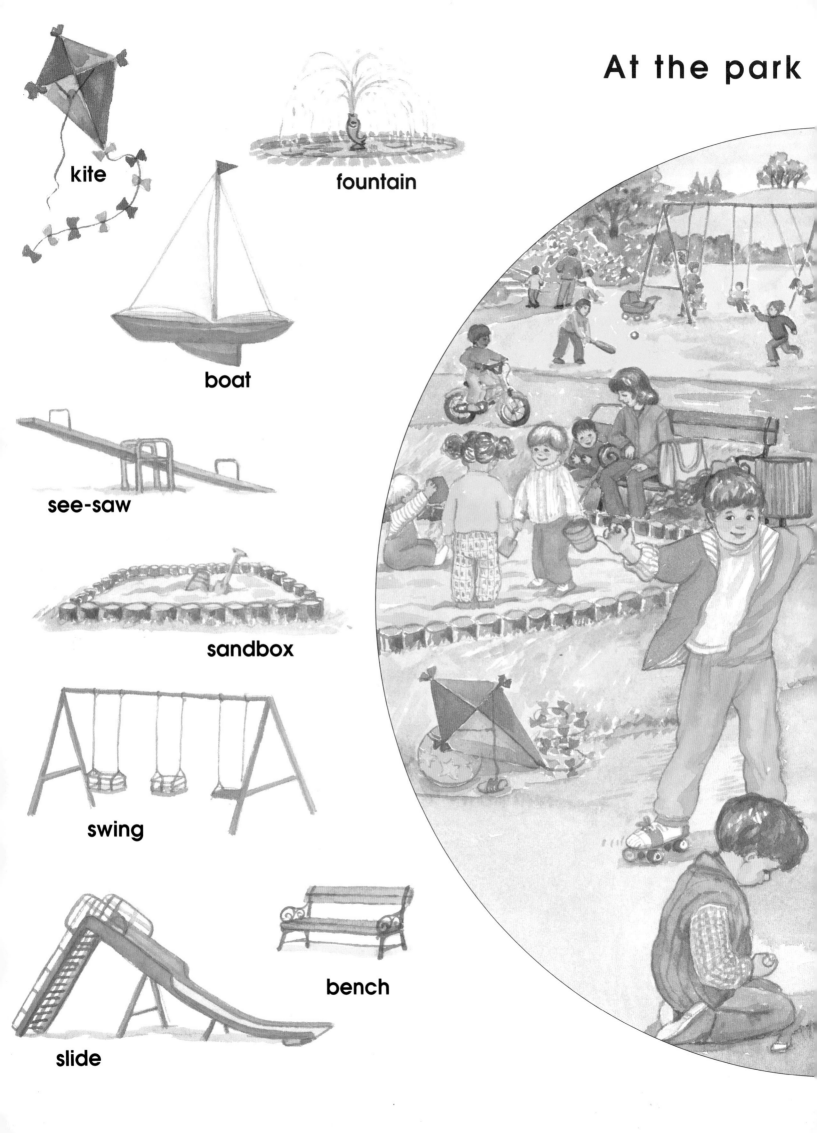

kite

fountain

boat

see-saw

sandbox

swing

slide

bench

At the park

scooter

rollerskates

marbles

bicycle

bat

ball

skateboard

Christmas tree

lights

tinsel

cards

holly

stocking

presents

mistletoe

angel

star

bell

belt

boots

beard

Santa Claus

reindeer

sleigh

lantern

fish

rabbit

bees

caterpillar

jar

tadpole

fishing pole

net

butterfly

By the river

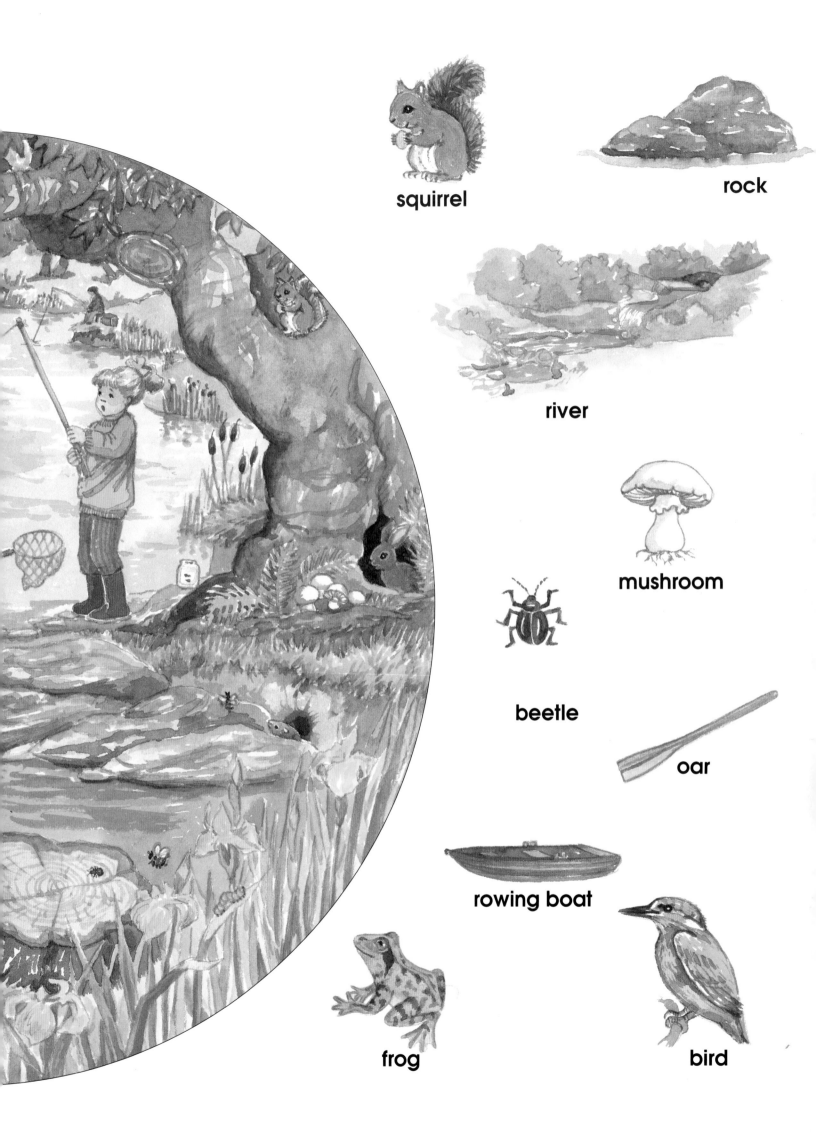

squirrel

rock

river

mushroom

beetle

oar

rowing boat

frog

bird

stars

slippers

comb

brush

mirror

pillow

bed

bath-tub

toothbrush

soap

sponge

quilt

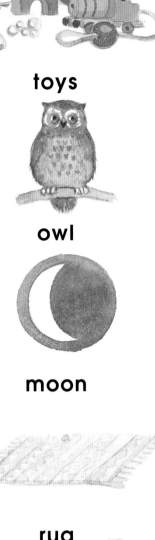

toys

owl

moon

rug

bubbles

toybox

  **storybook**

 **teddy bear**

sheet

towel

 **lamp**

What are they doing?

sliding

climbing

swinging

pushing

skating

pulling

skiing

jumping

running

hopping

skipping

swimming

rolling

throwing

What are they doing?

licking

painting

eating

drawing

drinking

writing

stirring

splashing

blowing

digging

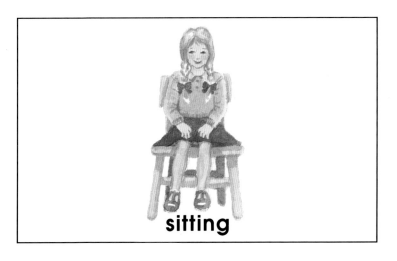

sitting

washing

standing

hanging